SNAKES

PYTHONS

James E. Gerholdt
ABDO & Daughters

Published by Abdo & Daughters, 4940 Viking Drive, Suite 622, Edina, Minnesota 55435.

Library bound edition distributed by Rockbottom Books, Pentagon Tower, P.O. Box 36036, Minneapolis, Minnesota 55435.

Printed in the United States.

Cover Photo credit: James Gerholdt
Interior Photo credits: Peter Arnold, Inc. pages 7, 9, 13, 17, 21
James Gerholdt, pages 5, 11, 15, 19

Edited by Julie Berg

Library of Congress Cataloging-in-Publication Data

Gerholdt, James E., 1943
        Pythons / James E. Gerholdt.
        p. cm. — (Snakes)
Includes bibliographical references and index.
Summary: Describes the physical characteristics, habitat, food habits, and defense mechanisms of this reptile which lives in jungles, rainforests, swampy areas, and even deserts.
ISBN 1-56239-517-3
1. Pythons—Juvenile literature. [1. Pythons. 2. Snakes.] I. Series: Gerholdt, James E., 1943- Snakes.
QL666.063G475   1995
597.96—dc20   95-4731
                                                                          CIP
                                                                          AC

About the Author

Jim Gerholdt has been studying reptiles and amphibians for more than 40 years. He has presented lectures and displays throughout the state of Minnesota for 9 years. He is a founding member of the Minnesota Herpetological Society and is active in conservation issues involving reptiles and amphibians in India and Aruba, as well as Minnesota.

Contents

PYTHONS

Pythons belong to one of the 11 snake families. There are about 25 python **species**. A snake is a **reptile**, which is a **vertebrate**. This means they have a backbone, just like a human.

Pythons are **cold blooded.** They get their body temperature from lying in the sun, on a warm log, or the warm ground. If they are too cool, their bodies won't work. If they get too hot, they will die. This is because their bodies need to be a certain temperature.

Like the boa **constrictors** and anacondas, pythons kill their prey by wrapping around it and squeezing until it **suffocates**.

Pythons kill their prey by wrapping around it and squeezing until it suffocates.

SIZES

Python species can be very large or small. Their length is measured from the tip of the nose to the tip of the tail. A **reticulated** python that was killed

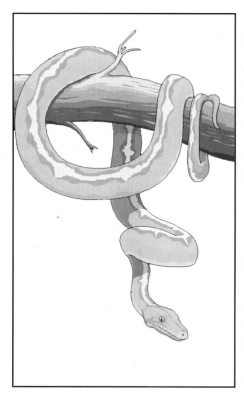

on the island of Celebes measured 33 feet (10 m). An African rock python killed in 1932 measured 32 feet (9.8 m). These are the only two python **species** that grow over 30 feet (9.1 m) long.

The amethystine python can be 22 feet (6.7 m) long. The Burmese python only reaches about 20 feet (6 m) in length.

A reticulated python from Indonesia.

The Mexican **burrowing** python is the smallest
species. It only reaches 4 feet (1.2 m) in length. A
very large python may weigh several hundred pounds
(136 kg).

COLORS

Pythons come in many colors. The green tree python from New Guinea and northern Australia is one of the prettiest and brightest-colored. The adults are a very bright green with small white markings on the back. The young may be yellow, brown, or red.

Another brightly colored **species** is the blood python from Borneo, Malaysia, and Sumatra. It is often a brick red color with uneven blotches. The Mexican **burrowing** python is a dark brown color with scattered light blotches.

Whether it is brightly colored or plain, the python's colors and markings help it blend in with its surroundings. This is called **camouflage**.

The green tree python from New Guinea and northern Australia is one of the brightest-colored snakes.

WHERE THEY LIVE

Pythons are found in many different **habitats**. Many live in jungles and **rainforests**. Some spend part of their time in trees.

The **reticulated** python is often found near houses and the nearby jungle. Other **species**, like the African rock python, live in forested and low brush areas. This species may also live near houses.

Some, like the blood python, like swampy areas. The Mexican **burrowing** python makes its home in the desert.

This reticulated python of Indonesia is wrapping itself around a tree.

WHERE THEY
ARE FOUND

Pythons are found all over the world. Africa is home to several python species, including the ball python. Australia probably has the most pythons, with about ten **species**. Borneo and New Guinea also have their share of pythons.

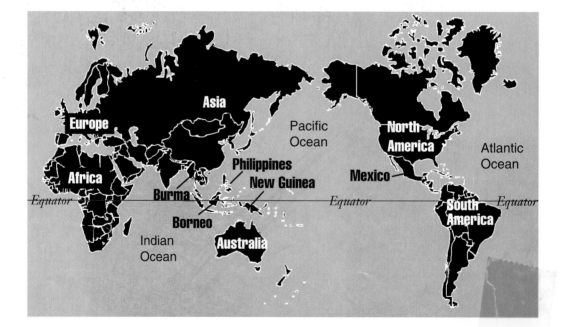

The African rock python enjoys the stony ground.

Asia and the Philippines are home to the largest python species, the **reticulated** python. The Burmese python, often seen in pet shops, comes from Southeast Asia. Only the Mexican **burrowing** python is found in the Americas.

SENSES

Pythons and humans share four of the same senses. But pythons have trouble seeing anything that isn't moving.

Their **pupils** are **vertical**, which helps them to see in the dark, when they are often active. These vertical pupils open up to let in more light.

Like all snakes, pythons have no ears and cannot hear. But they can feel **vibrations** through bones in the lower jaw.

The snake's most important sense **organ** is its tongue, with which they use to smell! Most pythons also have a row of heat-sensing pits on the upper jaw. These pits sense the body temperature of **warm-blooded prey**.

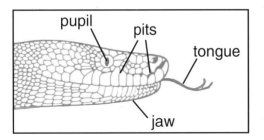

The green tree
python has
vertical pupils
which help it
to see
in the dark.

DEFENSE

The python's coloring and markings help it blend in with its surroundings. This **camouflage** is its most important defense against enemies. They include hyenas, crocodiles, jungle cats, and humans.

If the enemy can't see it, the python is safe. If a python is spotted by an enemy, it may try to crawl to a safe place, such as a hole or log. If this doesn't work, the python will **coil**, open its mouth, and hiss loudly. It may also strike and bite the enemy.

Though it is not **venomous**, the python has lots of sharp, needle-like teeth. The bite will hurt, but is not dangerous to humans.

Camouflage is the python's most important defense against enemies. This is a python from Australia.

FOOD

A hungry python will eat any bird or **mammal** it can swallow. An Indian python once killed and ate a large leopard! Sometimes **reptiles** and fish are also eaten.

The python catches its food by keeping still, hidden by its **camouflage**. When an animal comes close, the python strikes out and grabs its **prey** with its mouth. The sharp teeth hold on to the prey. Then the python **coils** around the animal and **constricts** it.

The constriction doesn't crush or break any bones. It **suffocates** the prey. Once the animal is dead, the python swallows it, usually head first.

This rock python is eating an impala. Notice the python's huge jaws as it swallows the animal.

BABIES

Baby pythons hatch from eggs laid by the female. Some **species**, like the African **burrowing** python, only lay two to four eggs. Others, like the **reticulated** python, can lay as many as 107!

Some female pythons **coil** around their eggs and **incubate** them. The mother can raise her body temperature by twitching her muscles.

Once the eggs have hatched, the babies go their own way. They shed their skin for the first time after seven to ten days. This is called **ecdysis**. It takes place whenever the old skin gets too small.

These baby Burmese pythons are hatching from their eggs.

GLOSSARY

Burrow (BIR-oh) - To dig into the ground.

Camouflage (CAM-a-flaj) - The ability to blend in with the surroundings.

Coil - To wind around into a pile, tube, or curl.

Cold-blooded - Animals that set their body temperature from an outside source.

Constrict - To make smaller or narrower by coiling.

Ecdysis (ek-DIE-sis) - The process of shedding the old skin.

Habitat (HAB-uh-tat) - The type of environment in which an animal lives.

Incubate (INK-u-bate) - To sit on eggs to hatch them.

Mammal (MAM-ull) - A warm-blooded animal with a backbone that nurses its young with milk.

Organ - Any part of an animal that is made up of different tissues and has a certain function.

Prey - Animals that are eaten by other animals.

Pupil (PEW-pill) - The opening in the eye's center where light enters.

Rainforest - A very thick forest in a place where rain is very heavy all through the year.

Reptile (REP-tile) - A scaly-skinned animal with a backbone.

Reticulated (ruh-TICK-u-lay-ted) - Having lines across the body that look like a net.

Species (SPEE-seas) - A kind or type.

Suffocate (SUFF-oh-kate) - To kill by stopping the breathing.

Venom (VEN-um) - Snake poison that is used to kill animals for food.

Vertebrate (VER-tuh-brit) - An animal with a backbone.

Vertical (VER-tih-kull) - Up and down.

Vibrations - A rapid movement back and forth.

Warm-blooded - Having blood that stays the same temperature no matter what the temperature is of the air or water around the animal.

BIBLIOGRAPHY

Mattison, Chris. *Snakes of the World.* Facts On File, Inc., 1991.

Obst, Fritz Jurgen, Klaus Richter, and Udo Jacob. *The Completely Illustrated Atlas of Reptiles and Amphibians for the Terrarium.* T.F.H. Publications, Inc., 1988.

Ross, Richard A. and Gerald Marzec. *The Reproductive Husbandry of Pythons and Boas.* Institute for Herpetological Research, 1990.

Stafford, Peter J. *Pythons and Boas.* T.F.H. Publications, Inc., 1986.

Index